RISING STARS

BRAIN ACADEMY
MATHS CHALLENGES

Mission File 5

Ages 10–12

Published in Association with
nace
National Association for Able Children in Education

Rising Stars are grateful to the following people for their support in developing this series: Sue Mordecai, Julie Fitzpatrick, Johanna Raffan and Belle Wallace.

NACE, The Core Business Centre, Milton Hill, Abingdon, Oxon OX13 6AB
www.nace.co.uk

Rising Stars Ltd, 7 Hatchers Mews, Bermondsey Street, London SE1 3GS
www.risingstars-uk.com

First edition published 2004
This edition published 2011

Written by: Charlotte Haggis, Louise Moore and Richard Cooper
Editorial consultants: Elaine Sellars, Sue Lowndes and Sally Harbour
Design: Burville-Riley
Illustrations: Cover and insides – Sue Lee / Characters – Bill Greenhead
Cover design: Burville-Riley Partnership

British Library Cataloguing in Publication Data
A CIP record for this book is available from the British Library.

ISBN (Trade): 978-1-84680-887-6
ISBN (Schools): 978-1-84680-902-6

Printed by Craft Print International Ltd.

CONTENTS

Welcome to Brain Academy!

Da Vinci

Da Vinci is the founder and head of the Brain Academy. He is all seeing, all thinking and all knowing – possibly the cleverest person alive. Nobody has ever actually seen him in the flesh as he communicates only via computer. When Da Vinci receives an emergency call for help, the members of Brain Academy jump into action (and that means you!).

Huxley

Huxley is Da Vinci's right-hand man. Not as clever, but still very smart. He is here to guide you through the missions and offer help and advice. The sensible and reliable face of Brain Academy, Huxley is cool under pressure.

Dr Hood

The mad doctor is the arch-enemy of Da Vinci and Brain Academy. He has set up a rival organisation called D.A.F.T. (which stands for Dull And Feeble Thinkers). Dr Hood and his agents will do anything they can to irritate and annoy the good people of this planet. He is a pain we could do without.

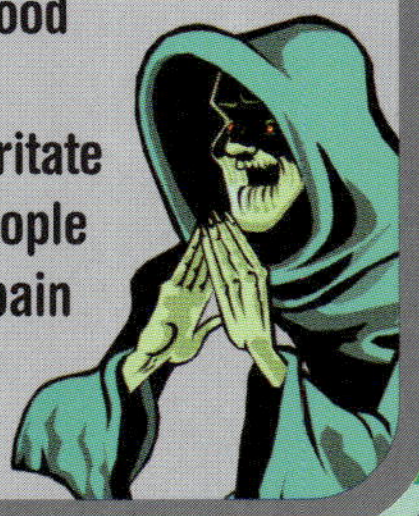

Hilary Kumar

Ms Kumar is the Prime Minister of our country. As the national leader she has a hotline through to the Academy but will only call in an extreme emergency. Confident and strong willed, she is a very tough cookie indeed.

General Cods-Wallop

This highly decorated gentleman (with medals, not wallpaper) is in charge of the armed forces. Most of his success has come from the help of Da Vinci and the Academy rather than the use of his somewhat limited military brain.

Mrs Tiggles

Stella Tiggles is the retired head of the Secret Intelligence service. She is a particular favourite of Da Vinci who treats her as his own mother. Mrs Tiggles' faithful companion is her cat, Bond… James Bond.

Maryland T. Wordsworth

M.T. Wordsworth is the president of the USA. Not the sharpest tool in the box, Maryland prefers to be known by his middle name, Texas, or 'Tex' for short. He takes great exception to being referred to as 'Mary' (which has happened in the past).

Buster Crimes

Buster is a really smooth dude and is in charge of the Police Force. His laid-back but efficient style has won him many friends, although these don't include Dr Hood or the agents of D.A.F.T. who regularly try to trick the coolest cop in town.

Sandy Buckett

The fearless Sandy Buckett is the head of the fire service. Sandy and her team of brave firefighters are always on hand, whether to extinguish the flames of chaos caused by the demented Dr Hood or just to rescue Mrs Tiggles' cat…

Echo the Eco-Warrior

Echo is the hippest chick around. Her love of nature and desire for justice will see her do anything to help an environmental cause – even if it means she's going to get her clothes dirty.

Victor Blastov

Victor Blastov is the leading scientist at the Space Agency. He once tried to build a rocket by himself but failed to get the lid off the glue. Victor often requires the services of the Academy, even if it's to set the video to record Dr Who.

Prince Barrington

Prince Barrington, or 'Bazza' as he is known to his friends, is the publicity-seeking heir to the throne. Always game for a laugh, the Prince will stop at nothing to raise money for worthy causes. A 'good egg' as his mother might say.

Working with Brain Academy

Do you get the idea? Now you've had the introduction we are going to show you the best way to use this book.

The plot

This tells you what the mission is about.

MISSION FILE 5:17

Buckett saves the skins of D.A.F.T. agents!

Time: 9.00am
Place: 'Bestgos' supermarket

A group of D.A.F.T. agents have decided to put a dampener on the summer barbecue season by stealing sausages from a well-known supermarket. They dug underneath the supermarket to take the store by surprise but have got stuck. Luckily, Sandy Buckett has been called to come and save their skins!

These D.A.F.T. thieves deserve a good grilling, but we need to save them first.

You can start the rescue mission by working on this Training Mission.

TM

It's going to take you a while to burrow through to the D.A.F.T. agents. Grab a spade and get shovelling at this conundrum.

1) If the fire brigade free one and a quarter D.A.F.T. agents in a day how many agents will they have rescued in FOUR weeks?

2) How many weeks and how many days would it take them to rescue 200 D.A.F.T. agents?

40

The Training Mission

Huxley will give you some practice before sending you on the main mission.

Each mission is divided up into different parts.

No one said this was easy. In fact that is why you have been chosen. Da Vinci will only take the best and he believes that includes you. Good luck!

Each book contains a number of 'missions' for you to take part in. You will work with the characters in Brain Academy to complete these missions.

The Main Mission

This is where you try to complete the challenge.

M1

Sandy is going to rescue the rest of the robbers but she needs your help to work out how long it will take.

1) If it takes Sandy's team a day and an eighth to uncover one whole and one eighth of an agent, how long would it take them to rescue 126 agents?

2) If they were to dig for one year and 20 weeks how many agents would they uncover?

3) How long would it take the fire brigade to uncover 504 D.A.F.T. agents?

Excellent! If Sandy can see this Da Vinci Challenge through, she'll uncover those undercover agents and hand them over to Buster Crimes.

Da Vinci files

Sandy needs to find the incriminating spades in order to get enough evidence to convict the D.A.F.T. agents. It takes her $\frac{4}{5}$ of a day to uncover $\frac{1}{8}$ of a spade.

1) How long would it take her to uncover TEN spades.

2) How many would she uncover in EIGHT weeks?

Huxley's Think Tank

If numbers are written as words and numerals, write them all as numerals. It is always useful to work out how long things would take with one spade.

41

The Da Vinci Files

These problems are for the best Brain Academy recruits. Very tough. Are you tough enough?

Huxley's Think Tank

Huxley will download some useful tips onto your PDA to help you on each mission.

PS: See pages 44–47 for a useful process and hints and tips!

A gang of thieves

Time: Just before tea
Place: BA headquarters

A group of D.A.F.T. agents are responsible for stealing thousands of dummies from the babies of Britain. Bawling babies are causing the nation's ears to ache and General Cods-Wallop has decided that he will be the one to stop the screaming, with a little help from Brain Academy of course!

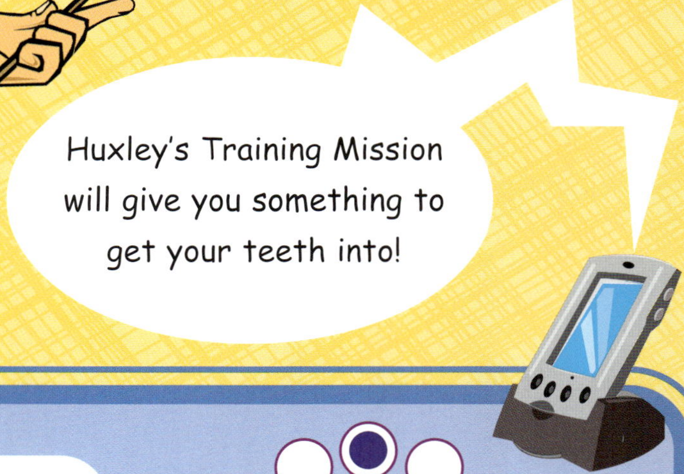

TM

A group of 13 D.A.F.T. agents have been brought in for questioning. The General has placed a blue hat on the head of the prime suspect so that he can remember to question this agent last. Can you help him work out where to start?

If he questions every THIRD agent where does he need to start if he is going to finish by questioning the crook in the blue hat?

M1

Some more thieves are brought in for questioning. Helping the General decide where to start will ensure that the dummies are returned to all those irate infants.

The General is standing in the middle of a circle of 15 D.A.F.T. agents. He has put the blue hat on the prime suspect as he wants to grill him last.

1) If he questions every FOURTH agent in the circle, where does he need to start in order to finish with the agent in blue?

2) Where should he start if he questions every ELEVENTH agent?

3) SIX more people join the circle. THREE sit on Blue hat's left and THREE sit on his right. Where should the General start if he questions every FIFTH agent and finishes with the agent in blue?

4) Where should he start if he questions every THIRTEENTH agent?

You've certainly proved you're no dummy! Completing the Da Vinci Challenge will ensure that the dummy thief is arrested and the babies can finally stop crying!

Da Vinci files

The General puts 12 chairs in a circle. He asks 150 suspects to line up and hands them a number sticker. He gives 1 to the FIRST, 2 to the SECOND and so on. Staying in their line they must then sit down on a chair or stand behind if it is occupied. The FIRST suspect sits on the chair at the 6 o'clock position, the next the 7 o'clock position and so on in a clockwise direction.

He will question every FIFTH group, moving in a clockwise direction. He wants to end with the group of villains who are standing at the 12 o'clock position.

1) Where must he start?

2) How many villains will be on or behind the 12 o'clock chair?

3) What numbers will their stickers show?

MISSION FILE 5:2

Building blocks

Time: 6.00am
Place: The Fire Station

Sandy Buckett's fire engines are refusing to start in the mornings. They get left outside in the cold overnight and she thinks they need to be kept warm to make sure they start first time. She needs the help of Brain Academy to design a block of six garages to house her temperamental trucks.

TM

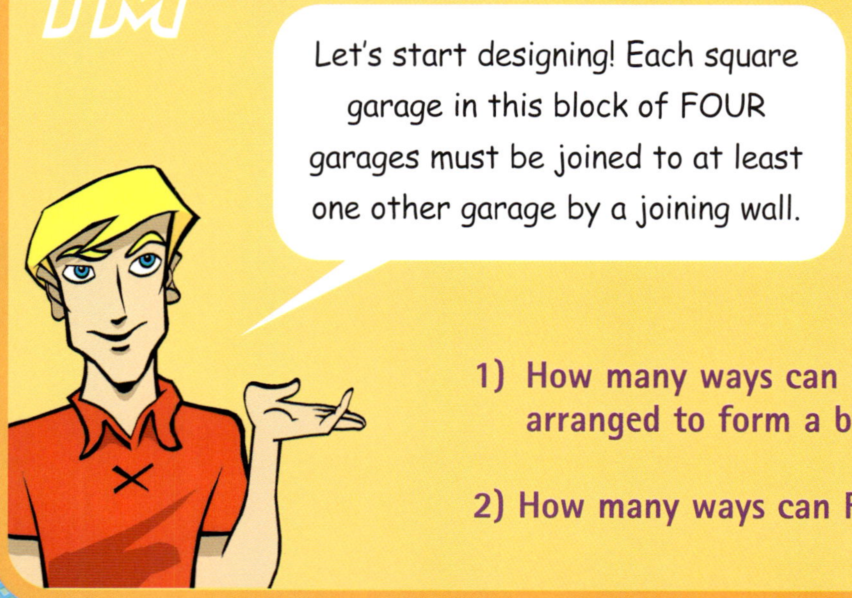

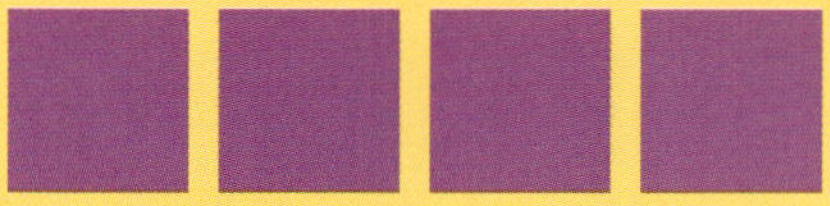

1) How many ways can FOUR garages be arranged to form a block?

2) How many ways can FIVE garages be arranged?

M1

Sandy is unsure which of the 4-block garages she should build. She needs your help to work out the basic cost of each block.

Each individual garage measures 25m x 25m. An external wall for one side of one garage costs £1,500. A door covers the entire wall and costs £1,400. Fire engines only reverse straight back into the garage or drive forwards out of the garage (they can't manoeuvre in the garages). For security reasons, there must be the least number of doors possible.

1) Which of the designs for a FOUR-block garage would be cheapest to build?

2) If Sandy chose this design rather than the most expensive option, how much would she save?

3) How much would the most expensive FIVE-unit garage block cost Sandy?

4) If Sandy chose this design rather than the cheapest option, how much extra would she spend?

Marvellous! As soon as Sandy completes the Da Vinci Challenge she won't have to worry about mis-firing engines again!

Da Vinci files

Investigate the prices of an SIX-unit garage. What are your findings?

"Cheers, General!"

Time: Dinner time
Place: British Army kitchen

General Cods-Wallop has decided it's time to take action and save children from irritable and grumpy parents. He has decided to concoct a potion that will make even the most temperamental parents smile and laugh after just one sip. He will need a little help from Brain Academy of course!

TM

CHICKEN CURRY
Makes 1.5 kg

Two chicken portions (same weight)
The same weight of gravy powder
Same weight of onions
Half the weight of the chicken in curry powder
A quarter of the weight of the chicken in chillies (fresh)

1) How much does ONE chicken portion weigh?
2) What weight of onions is needed to make 2.25 kg of curry?
3) If a batch of curry is made which uses FOUR times the weight of chillies, what weight of gravy will be needed?

M1

Ready, steady, cook, General Cods-Wallop is ready to make the potion. Answering these questions will be sure to get those grumpy parents grinning.

CHEER

Measure 4 jugs of a sports energy drink.
Next, measure exactly the same quantity of fresh spring water.
Stir in half this quantity of lemonade.
You will need the same amount of apple juice as lemonade.
Add 2 jugs of cod liver oil mixture.
Add half the quantity of apple juice in vegetable oil.
You should pour all the mixture into 12 airtight containers, pouring 180 ml into each.

1) How many ml of sports energy drink went into the mixture?

2) To make half the quantity of CHEER, how much vegetable oil is needed?

3) If one jug of cod liver oil is used, how many ml of spring water will be needed?

4) To make 6.48 litres of the mixture, how much of each ingredient is needed?

Well done! Completing the Da Vinci Challenge will make sure those parents stay happy all the time.

Da Vinci files

When the General made a batch of CHEER he used 1,280 ml of sports drink.

1) How much mixture would he pour into each of the 12 bottles when he'd finished?

2) How much apple juice went into this?

MISSION FILE 5:4

A [pond] sample question!

Time: Just before lunch
Place: A slimy pond

The people of Frogsbourne, are extremely concerned about a strange green slime that has appeared on the surface of its six lovely ponds. Can you help Echo to take samples from the ponds so that she can help detect what might be causing this nasty goo?

TM

You must measure 10 quantities of pond water in full litres from 1 to 10 litres. You are only allowed THREE containers. Each container must hold a certain number of complete litres. The first container has a capacity of 1 litre, the second 3 litres and the third 6 litres. Each container can only be used once in collecting each quantity.

1) How can Echo use the three containers to measure quantities from 1 litre to 10 litres inclusively?

2) Find another combination of three containers which could have been used for the job.

M1

Echo now needs to measure a quantity of water from ONE of the ponds. To her horror she realises that she has picked up the wrong containers. She's going to need your help if she is to collect enough samples to find out the cause of this slime.

1) She needs to measure 2 litres of water using a 3-litre container and a 1-litre container. Can she measure 2 litres using these two containers?

2) Echo wants to measure 4 litres but in her hurry she picks up a 5-litre and a 3-litre container. Is it possible to measure 4 litre using these containers?

3) Echo wants to measure 6 litres of pond water. Is this possible if she picks up a 5-litre and a 7-litre container?

4) Is it possible to measure 8 litres using a 7-litre and a 9-litre container?

Fabulous work! If Echo is to ensure that these ponds remain free of this revolting slime, she'll need to complete the Da Vinci Challenge.

Da Vinci files

Echo decides to tip some of the water into an empty rectangular based bottle.
When she gets home she realises that she does not have any measuring cylinders which would allow her to measure the volume. The only thing she has is a ruler.

1) What would she need to know in order to use the ruler to find the volume in ml of water?
2) How would she calculate the volume of the bottle?
3) If the base of the bottle was round, how would she work out the volume of this partially filled bottle?

A blaze of glory for Sandy's firefighters

Time: Late morning
Place: Sandy Buckett's garden

Sandy Buckett has sponsored five of her female firefighters in a charity fun run to raise money for their local hospital. They each wore fancy dress to complete the 9-mile race and were pleased to finish in the top five places, especially as they all incurred an injury on the way. Sandy is a little confused about where each one was placed. She needs the help of Brain Academy to work out how much she should pay each one.

TM

1) Charlotte arrived before Jenny. Maureen arrived after Charlotte. Anne arrived after Maureen but not last.

2) Smith changed more slowly than Jones. Best was slower than Potts. Smith beat Potts into her costume.

M1

Now find out the first and surnames of the FIVE ladies, where they finished in the race, what they dressed up as and what injury they picked up along the way. On your marks, get set, go!

Maureen injured her back.
She finished behind the lady who hurt her leg.
Green came as a bear and injured her foot.
She did not come in fifth place.
The lady who injured her knee was fourth to finish and came as Robin Hood.
Sarah Potts came in at an odd number and hated dragons.
The lady with the bad back came as a school girl, finished next to Charlotte and finished ahead of the lady with the bad knee.
Smith was the third lady to finish and she came two places in front of Potts.
Anne beat Jenny and Maureen.
Maureen was not married to Mr Best. She was not Harry Potter.
The person who came fifth went home with a big bandage on their ankle.
Jones finished behind the lady with the hurt foot and in front of the schoolgirl.

Completing the Da Vinci Challenge will allow Sandy to give each fire fighter the right money for their chosen charity.

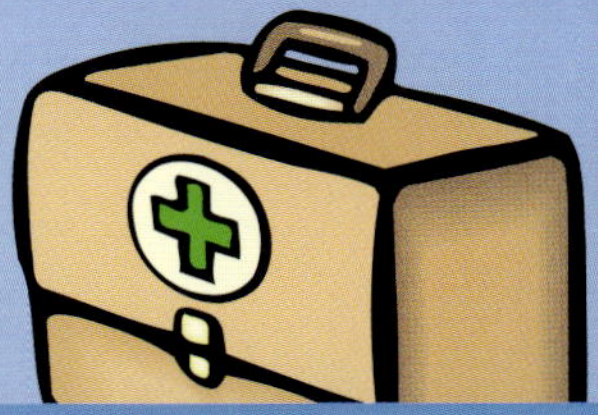

Da Vinci files

1) Charlotte was sick on the day of the race meaning that she was unable to compete. Rewrite the sentences above that are no longer true so that the story is accurate.

2) Anne and Sarah are unable to compete. Can you rewrite the story for the remaining THREE runners?

3) Have a go at creating your own problem. It is essential that you provide enough information. You also need to avoid any unnecessary statements.

A hair-raising problem

Time: Early afternoon
Place: Old MacDonald's Farm

A group of D.A.F.T. agents have been secretly manufacturing wigs to sell at the N.A.F.C (National Association for the Follically Challenged) summer fête next month. Unfortunately, the burning of the wool and the glue, which causes a harmful smoke, is causing the animals on a nearby farm to become very sick! Old MacDonald has asked Echo the Eco-Warrior for her help.

TM

1) Echo counted 90 wigs. ONE THIRD of them were blond, FOUR TENTHS of them were black and FOUR FIFTEENTHS of them were brown. How many of each colour did she find?

2) In a second room she counted 200 wigs. ONE QUARTER of them were clown wigs, FIVE EIGHTHS of them were Rapunzel wigs and TWO SIXTEENTHS were judge's wigs. How many of each did she find?

M1

Echo needs to find out how many animals have become ill if she is going to try and save them, but she needs your help.

1) Old MacDonald had sheep, cows and pigs, and he told Echo that ONE QUARTER of the animals were sheep and TWO THIRDS were cows. He has TWELVE pigs. How many animals does Old MacDonald have?

2) Old MacDonald tells Echo that he also has a farm with THREE other types of animal where THREE FIFTHS of the animals are horses and ONE EIGHTH are chickens. If he has 44 goats how many animals does Old MacDonald have on the second farm?

Excellent work. If Echo is to save all the animals she must tackle the Da Vinci Challenge.

Da Vinci files

"Your farm must be huge with all those animals in it," said Echo.

"It is," agreed Old MacDonald "It's ten kilometres square, or should I say ten square kilometres. They both mean the same thing after all!"

Do you agree with Old MacDonald? Explain your answer.

Inventions for beginners

Time: Lunchtime
Place: NASA headquarters

Struggling inventor, Professor Noel Ogic, is at his wits' end. He just can't seem to get any of his inventions to work. His paper kettle was a flop and his wooden scissors just didn't cut it with anyone! Luckily for Noel, Victor Blastov has agreed to help him and has dug out his copy of the best-selling book *Inventions for Beginners: Volume I.*

TM

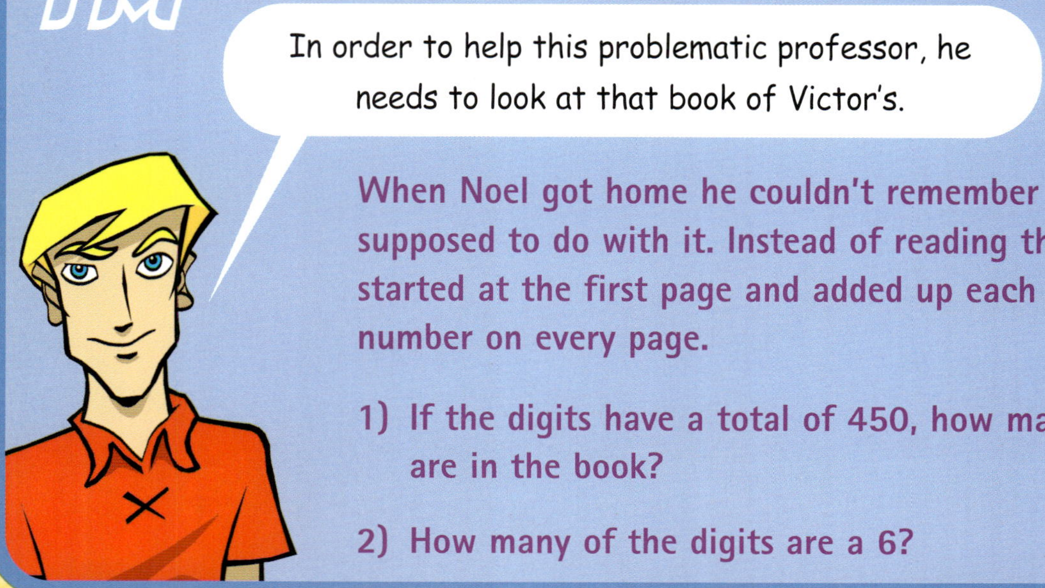

When Noel got home he couldn't remember what he was supposed to do with it. Instead of reading the book, Noel started at the first page and added up each digit of each page number on every page.

1) If the digits have a total of 450, how many pages are in the book?

2) How many of the digits are a 6?

M1

Inventing ingenious inventions is a big task. The professor will need to read Volume II if he wants to be a success!

Again, the hapless inventor added the digits on each page and found the total was 703.

1) How many pages are there in Volume II?

2) The professor realised he hadn't counted the final chapter. He totalled up these digits and found that the total for this part was 279. How many pages are there altogether in Volume II?

3) How many of the digits are a 4?

Great! If Victor can complete the Da Vinci Challenge, Noel will be sure to make millions from his next invention!

Da Vinci files

Volume III has 99 pages. If you add up each digit on each page what will the total be?

MISSION FILE 5:8

A chocolate bar challenge

Time: Snack time
Place: Stella Tiggles' house

D.A.F.T. agents are causing misery amongst millions by misdirecting lorry-loads of chocolate bars from sweet shops all over the country. Mrs Stella Tiggles has just one bar of chocolate left in her cupboard. She needs to call Brain Academy if she's going to make it last.

TM

Stella has a chocolate bar made of EIGHT delicious small square chunks. She decides to break off a square of this 2 x 4 bar as a little treat. She realises there are 11 ways that she can break off a square of chocolate. Helping Mrs Tiggles to count squares will allow her pass the Training Mission and eat chocolate for a few days!

1) **How many squares can be counted in a 2 x 2 chocolate bar made up of FOUR square chunks?**

2) **How many squares can be counted in a 4 x 3 chocolate bar made up of 12 square chunks?**

M1

If Stella can count the squares in these bars of chocolate she will be able to carry on eating chocolate for another week.

1) How many squares can be counted in a 3 x 3 chocolate bar made up of 9 square chunks?

2) How many squares can be counted in a 4 x 4 chocolate bar?

3) Investigate the squares that can be counted in other SQUARE chocolate bars. Start with a 5 x 5 bar. Do you notice any patterns or rules?

4) Can you use the patterns you have found to predict how many squares can be seen in a square bar of chocolate made up of 169 square chunks?

Completing the Da Vinci Challenge will mean Stella can keep eating chocolate for a whole month.

Da Vinci files

Investigate RECTANGULAR chocolate bars with a height of TWO squares and then THREE squares. Describe any patterns that you notice.

You could extend your investigation to rectangular chocolate bars with other heights.

MISSION FILE 5:9

Stella hits the jackpot!

Time: After bedtime
Place: Mrs Tiggles' bedroom

Mrs Tiggles is lying in bed imagining all the things she would be able to buy if she won the lottery. To try to get some sleep, she starts counting sheep… 56, 57, 58… Suddenly she sits bolt upright in bed, "That's it," she shouts, "these sheep are the answer to my prayers!" Stella believes that by choosing consecutive numbers when she plays the lottery, she will be sure to win the jackpot!

TM

If you can help Mrs Tiggles choose her numbers she'll stand a good chance of winning £10.00 in next Wednesday's draw.

1) Which TWO consecutive numbers can be added together to give Mrs Tiggles' door number, 85?
2) Can 85 be made by adding THREE, FOUR and FIVE consecutive numbers?
3) Are there strings of consecutive numbers that total 84 (her cousin Bella's age)?
4) What is the maximum amount of consecutive numbers, that total 84?

Brain Academy Maths Challenges Mission File 5
Answer booklet

Welcome to Brain Academy Maths! Designed for children who enjoy a challenge, the five Brain Academy books provide a wealth of fun activities and investigations. Suitable for children working at slightly beyond the expected National Curriculum level for their age, all the activities help support the current National Curriculum which can be found at http://curriculum.qcda.gov.uk. Are you and your child ready to become a member of Brain Academy? Remember to look at Huxley's Think Tank for a helpful hint when the pressure is on and work systematically. Good luck!

MISSION FILE 5:1 A gang of thieves

TM Remember, the General only needs to question each person once.

Start 3rd person from blue in a clockwise direction.

M1

1) Start 6th person from blue in a clockwise direction.
2) Start 14th person from blue in a clockwise direction.
3) Start 14th person from blue in a clockwise direction.
4) Start 4th person from blue in a clockwise direction.

Da Vinci files

1) Start at the 4 o'clock position.
2) One sat on the chair and eleven stood behind (12 in all).
3) Numbers 7, 19, 31, 43, 55, 67, 79, 91, 103, 115, 127, 139

MISSION FILE 5:2 Building blocks

Squared paper will be useful for this mission.

TM

1) 5 basic shapes can be made. These are called tetrominoes. If rotations and reflections are allowed, more ways can be found.

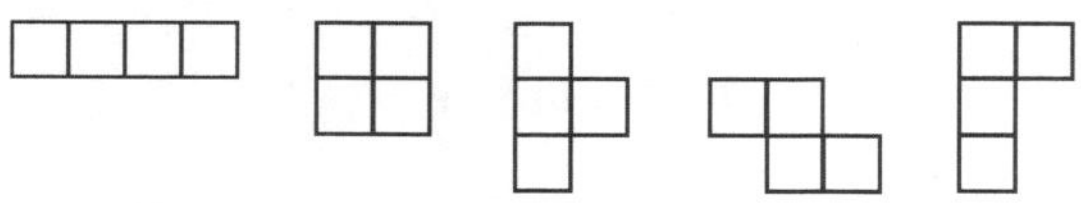

2) These 12 shapes are known as pentominoes. If reflections and rotations of these shapes are allowed, rather more ways are possible.

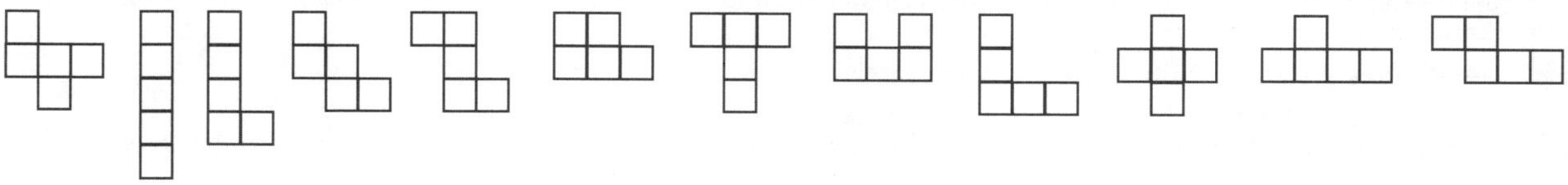

M1

1) 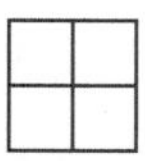

Cheapest = 2 doors + 6 external walls = £2800 + £9000 = £11 800

2) 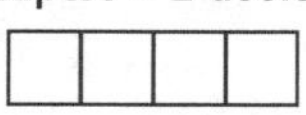

Most expensive = 1 door + 9 external walls = £14 900
Saved £14 900 - £11 800 = £3100

3) 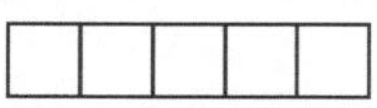

Most expensive = 1 door + 11 external walls = £1400 + £16 500 = £17 900

4) 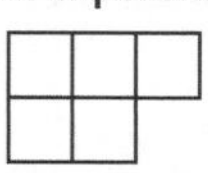

Cheapest = 2 doors + 8 external walls = £2800 + £12 000 = £14 800
Extra spent = £17 900 - £14 800 = £3100

Da Vinci files

Cheapest = £14 800
Most expensive = £20 900
Difference = £6100

MISSION FILE 5:3 "Cheers, General!"

TM

The weight of the gravy powder is the same as the total weight of the chicken portions, so $7\frac{1}{2}$ units of weight = 1500 g,
1 unit = 200 g

1) 200 g
2) 600 g
3) 1600 g

M1

12 containers x 180 ml = 2160 ml   15 jugs = 2160 ml so 1 jug = 144 ml

1) 576 ml
2) 72 ml
3) 288 ml
4) 12 jugs (1728 ml) sports energy drink
   12 jugs (1728 ml) fresh spring water
   6 jugs (864 ml) lemonade
   6 jugs (864 ml) apple juice
   6 jugs (864 ml) cod-liver oil mixture
   3 jugs (432 ml) vegetable oil

Da Vinci files

1280 ÷ 4 = 320 ml per jug   Total = 320 x 15 jugs = 4800 ml

1) 400 ml
2) 640 ml

MISSION FILE 5:4 A [pond] sample question!

TM

1) 1 litre, 3 litre and 6 litre containers
   1 litre = 1 litre 2 = 3 − 1 3 = 3 4 = 3 + 1 5 = 6 - 1 6 = 6 7 = 6 + 1 8 = 6 + 3 - 1 9 = 6 + 3
   10 = 6 + 3 + 1
2) 1 litre, 2 litres and 7 litres
   1 = 1 2 = 2 3 = 2 + 1 4 = 7 - 2 - 1 5 = 7 - 2 6 = 7 - 1 7 = 7 8 = 7 + 1 9 = 7 + 2
   10 = 7 + 2 + 1

M1

1) Fill the 3-litre container from the pond, fill the 1-litre container from the 3-litre container so there are 2 litres left in the 3-litre container.

   Pond ⟶ 3 litres − 1 litre = 2 litres left in 3-litre container
2) Pond ⟶ 5 litres − 3 litres = 2 litres left in 5-litre container
   Throw the contents of the 3-litre container back in the pond and put the 2 litres from the 5-litre container into the 3-litre container.
   Pond ⟶ 5-litre container − 1 litre to fill up the 3-litre container = 4 litres left in 5-litre container.
3) Pond ⟶ 7 litres − 5 litres = 2 litres left in 7-litre container
   Empty the 5-litre container back into the pond.
   Put the 2 remaining litres into the 5-litre container.
   Pond ⟶ 7 litres − 3 litres to fill the 5-litre container = 4 litres left in 7-litre container.
   Empty the 5-litre container back into the pond.
   Put the 4 remaining litres into the 5-litre container.
   Pond ⟶ 7 litres − 1 litre to fill the 5-litre container = 6 litres left in 7-litre container.
4) Pond ⟶ 9 litres − 7 litres = 2 litres left in 9-litre container
   Empty the 7-litre container back into the pond.
   Put the 2 remaining litres into the 7-litre container.
   Pond ⟶ 9 litres − 5 litres to fill the 7-litre container = 4 litres left in 9-litre container.
   Empty the 7-litre container back into the pond.
   Put the 4 remaining litres into the 7-litre container.
   Pond ⟶ 9 litres − 3 litres to fill the 7-litre container = 6 litres left in 9-litre container.
   Empty the 7-litre container back into the pond.
   Put the 6 remaining litres into the 7-litre container.
   Pond ⟶ 9 litres − 1 litre to fill the 7-litre container = 8 litres left in 9-litre container.

Da Vinci files

1) Use the knowledge that $1 cm^3 = 1 ml$.
2) Use the ruler to measure the length, depth and breadth and multiply them together.
3) Find the area of the base (using the formula $\pi r2$) and multiply by the height of the bottle.

MISSION FILE 5:5 A blaze of glory for Sandy's firefighters

TM

1) 1st: Charlotte 2nd: Maureen 3rd: Anne 4th: Jenny
2) 1st: Jones 2nd: Smith 3rd: Potts 4th: Best

ML

Maureen				Sarah				Charlotte				Anne				Jenny			
1st	Best	Knee	RH	1st	Best	Knee	RH	1st	Best	Knee	RH	**1st**	Best	Knee	RH	1st	**Best**	**Knee**	**RH**
2nd	Green	**Back**	D	2nd	Green	Back	D	**2nd**	Green	Back	**D**	2nd	**Green**	Back	D	2nd	Green	Back	D
3rd	Potts	Leg	**SG**	3rd	**Potts**	Leg	SG	3rd	Potts	**Leg**	SG	3rd	Potts	Leg	SG	3rd	Potts	Leg	SG
4th	**Smith**	Ankle	HP	4th	Smith	**Ankle**	**HP**	4th	Smith	Ankle	HP	4th	Smith	Ankle	HP	**4th**	Smith	Ankle	HP
5th	Jones	Foot	B	**5th**	Jones	Foot	B	5th	**Jones**	Foot	B	5th	Jones	**Foot**	**B**	5th	Jones	Foot	B

Da Vinci files

1) Change the eight sentences to:
(Maureen) finished behind the lady who hurt her foot.
(Green) did not finish in 4th place.
The lady who injured her knee was 3rd to finish and came as Robin Hood.
Sarah Potts came in as an even number and hated dragons.
The lady with the bad back came as a schoolgirl and finished ahead of the lady with the bad knee.
Smith was the second lady to finish and came two places in front of Potts.
The person who came in 4th went home with a big bandage on their ankle.
The lady with the hurt foot finished in front of the schoolgirl.

2) Maureen injured her back.
She finished behind the lady who hurt her leg.
The lady who injured her knee was third to finish and came as Robin Hood.
The lady with the bad back came as a schoolgirl, finished next to Charlotte and finished ahead of the lady with the bad knee.
Smith was the second lady to finish.
Maureen was not married to Mr Best. She was not Harry Potter.
Jones finished in front of the schoolgirl and her bad leg didn't seem to slow her down at all.

MISSION FILE 5:6 A hair-raising problem for Echo

TM

1) 30 blonde, 36 black, 24 brown
2) 50 clown wigs, 125 Rapunzel wigs, 25 judges' wigs

ML

1) $\frac{1}{4} + \frac{2}{3} = \frac{3}{12} + \frac{8}{12} \rightarrow \frac{11}{12}$ so pigs $\rightarrow \frac{1}{12} \rightarrow 12$
So total 144 animals

2) $\frac{3}{5} + \frac{1}{8} = \frac{24}{40} + \frac{5}{40} = \frac{29}{40}$ so goats $\rightarrow \frac{11}{40} \rightarrow 44$ and $\frac{1}{40} \rightarrow 4$
So total animals = 4 x 40 = 160 animals

Da Vinci files

The wording is ambiguous and it may imply that 'ten kilometres square' is a square with sides of 10km giving an area of 10 x 10 = 100km^2.

'Ten square kilometres' is an area which 10 square kilometres would cover (e.g. a rectangle with sides of 2km and 5km).

MISSION FILE 5:7 Inventions for beginners

TM

Use the fact that the numbers 1 to 9 add up to 45.

1) 45 + (45 + 10) + (45 + 20) + (45 + 30) + (45 + 40) + (45 + 50) + 6 + 0 + 6 + 1 + 6 + 2 + 6 + 3 = 63
2) 10 digits are a 6 (in the numbers 6, 16, 26, 36, 46, 56, 60, 61, 62, 63)

ML

1) 85
2) 30 + 85 = 115
3) 22, in the numbers 4, 14, 24, 34, 40, 41, 42, 43, 44, 45, 46, 47, 48, 49, 54, 64, 74, 84, 94, 104, 114

Da Vinci files

900

MISSION FILE 5:8 A chocolate bar challenge

TM

1) 5 (1 + 4)   2) 20

M1

1) 14 (1 + 4 + 9)
2) 30 (1 + 4 + 9 + 16)
3) The total is always the sum of square numbers.
For a 7 square the total is 140 = $7^2 + 6^2 + 5^2 + 4^2 + 3^2 + 2^2 + 1^2$

	1 x 1 squares in it	2 x 2 squares in it	3 x 3 squares in it	4 x 4 squares in it	5 x 5 squares in it	6 x 6 squares in it	7 x 7 squares in it	Total squares
1 square	1							1
2 square	4	1						5
3 square	9	4	1					14
4 square	16	9	4	1				30
5 square	25	16	9	4	1			55
6 square	36	25	16	9	4	1		91
7 square	49	36	25	16	9	4	1	140

4) $13^2 = 169$
13 square contains: 169 + 144 + 121 + 100 + 81 + 64 + 49 + 36 + 25 + 16 + 9 + 4 + 1 = 819

Da Vinci files

	1 x 1 squares in it	2 x 2 squares in it	Total squares
2 x 2 square	4	1	5
2 x 3 rectangle	6	2	8
2 x 4 rectangle	8	3	11
2 x 5 rectangle	10	4	14
2 x 6 rectangle	12	5	17
2 x 7 rectangle	14	6	20

Patterns include single squares increasing in twos, 2 x 2 squares increasing in ones and the total increasing in threes (the two + one).

	1 x 1 squares in it	2 x 2 squares in it	3 x 3 squares in it	Total squares in it
3 x 2 rectangle	6	2	0	8
3 x 3 square	9	4	1	14
3 x 4 rectangle	12	6	2	20
3 x 5 rectangle	15	8	3	26
3 x 6 rectangle	18	10	4	32
3 x 7 rectangle	21	12	5	38

Patterns include single squares increasing in threes, 2 x 2 squares increasing in twos, 3 x 3 squares increasing in ones and the total increasing in sixes (the three + two + one).

MISSION FILE 5:9 Stella hits the jackpot

TM

To discover if a total can be made by a specified number of consecutive numbers, divide the total by the number of consecutive numbers. An odd number of consecutive numbers must divide without a remainder, an even number must end with □.5. Once the answer to this division sum is less than half the divisor, leave the calculation.

1) 42, 43
2) 85 ÷ 3 = 28.333, so it can not be made with three consecutive numbers
85 ÷ 4 = 21.25, so it can not be made with four consecutive numbers
85 ÷ 5 = 17, so the consecutive numbers are 15, 16, 17, 18, 19
3) 84 ÷ 2 = 42, not two consecutives
84 ÷ 3 = 28, three consecutives are 27, 28, 29
84 ÷ 4 = 21, not four consecutives
84 ÷ 5 = 16.8, not five consecutives
84 ÷ 6 = 14, not six consecutives
84 ÷ 7 = 12, so seven consecutives are 9, 10, 11, 12, 13, 14, 15
84 ÷ 8 = 10.5, so eight consecutives are 7, 8, 9, 10, 11, 12, 13, 14
84 ÷ 9 = 9.333..., not nine consecutives
84 ÷ 10 = 8.4, not ten consecutives
84 ÷ 11 = 7.63... not eleven consecutives
84 ÷ 12 = 7, not twelve consecutives
84 ÷ 13 = 6.46... which is less than half of 13 so stop investigation here
4) 8

MI

1) Four consecutives are 34, 35, 36, 37
2) Twelve consecutives are 10, 11, 12, 13, 14, 15, 16, 17, 18, 19, 20, 21
3) Eighteen consecutives are 5, 6, 7, 8, 9, 10, 11, 12, 13, 14, 15, 16, 17, 18, 19, 20, 21, 22
4) Two consecutives are 183, 184

Da Vinci files

1) The numbers 1 – 140 added together (i.e. 140 consecutive numbers) total 9870
2) 1 x 2 x 3 x 4 x 5
3) Maximum for 3 digit numbers is 1 – 6 (ie; 6 consecutive numbers) 1 x 2 x 3 x 4 x 5 x 6 = 720
   Maximum for 4 digit numbers is 1 – 7 (ie; 7 consecutive numbers) 1 x 2 x 3 x 4 x 5 x 6 x 7 = 5040
   Maximum for 5 digit numbers is 1 – 8 (ie; 8 consecutive numbers) 1 x 2 x 3 x 4 x 5 x 6 x 7 x 8 = 40320
   Maximum for 6 digit numbers is 1 – 9 (ie; 9 consecutive numbers) 1 x 2 x 3 x 4 x 5 x 6 x 7 x 8 x 9 = 362880

MISSION FILE 5:10 On your bike, Tex!

TM

1) 8 blips (112, 121, 126, 134, 137, 143, 162, 173)
2) 6 blips (115, 135, 151, 153, 157, 175)

MI

1) Zero
2) 34 ways
   (100, 101, 102, 103, 104, 105, 106, 107, 108, 109, 110, 120, 125, 130, 140, 145, 150, 152, 154, 155, 156, 158, 159, 160, 165, 169, 170, 178, 180, 185, 187, 190, 195, 196)

3) Three-digit blips	4) Four-digit blips	5) Five-digit blips	Six-digit blips
0 – 425	0 - 4607	0 -58796	0 - 562374
1 – 111	1 – 1111	1 – 11111	1 - 111111
2 – 317	2 – 6112	2 – 21312	2 - 611211
3 – 311	3 – 3111	3 – 11113	3 - 311111
4 – 981	4 – 3133	4 – 32223	4 - 212233
5 – 531	5 – 5315	5 – 55131	5 - 151531
6 – 681	6 – 2342	6 – 23462	6 - 223221
7 – 711	7 – 1171	7 – 17111	7 - 711111
8 – 617	8 – 3223	8 – 96422	8 - 892348
9 – 331	9 – 3131	9 - 33111	9 - 311311

(There may be alternative answers to these)

Da Vinci files

Consecutive numbers:

Three-digits	Four-digits	Five-digits	Six-digits	Seven-digits
123 = 6	1234 = 8	12345 = 0	123456 = 0	1234567 = 0
234 = 8	2345 = 0	23456 = 0	234567 = 0	2345678 = 0
345 = 0	3456 = 0	34567 = 0	345678 = 0	3456789 = 0
456 = 0	4567 = 0	45678 = 0	456789 = 0	
567 = 0	5678 = 0	56789 = 0		
678 = 0	6789 = 0			
789 = 0				

Consecutive numbers containing the digits 5 or above give blips of zero.

MISSION FILE 5:11 Rows and rows of roses

TM

1) 5 square + 3 square = 25 + 9 = 34
2) 6 square + 6 square = 36 + 36 = 72
3) 10 square + 4 square = 100 + 16 = 116

MI

1)

1+ 4 = 5	1 + 9 = 10	1 + 16 = 17	1 + 25 = 26	1 + 36 = 37	1 + 49 = 100	1 + 64 = 65	1 + 81 = 91	4 + 9 = 13
4 + 16 = 20	4 + 25 = 29	4 + 36 = 40	4 + 49 = 53	4 + 64 = 68	4 + 81 = 85	9 + 16 = 25	9 + 25 = 34	9 + 36 = 45
9 + 49 = 58	9 + 64 = 73	9 + 81 = 90	16 + 25 = 41	16 + 36 = 52	16 + 49 = 65	16 + 64 = 80	16 + 81 = 97	25 + 36 = 61
25 + 49 = 74	25 + 64 = 89	36 + 49 = 85	36 + 64 = 100					

Numbers that can be made are 5, 10, 13, 17, 20, 25, 26, 29, 34, 37, 40, 41, 45, 52, 53, 58, 61, 65, 68, 73, 74, 80, 85, 89, 90, 91, 97, 100.

2) By working systematically, in order, through the possibilities.

Da Vinci files

1+4+9=14	1+4+16=21	1+4+25=30	1+4+36=41	1+4+49=54	1+4+64=69	1+4+81=86	1+9+16=26
1+9+25=35	1+9+36=46	1+9+49=59	1+9+64=74	1+9+81=91	1+16+25=42	1+16+36=53	1+16+49=66
1+16+64=81	1+16+81=98	1+25+36=62	1+25+49=75	1+25+64=90	1+36+49=86	4+9+64=77	4+9+81=94
4+9+16=29	4+9+25=38	4+9+36=49	4+9+49=62	4+25+36=65	4+25+49=78	4+16+25=45	4+16+36=56
4+16+49=69	4+16+64=84	9+16+49=74	9+16+64=89	4+25+64=93	4+36+49=89	9+16+25=50	9+16+36=61
16+25+36=77	16+25+49=90	9+25+36=70	9+25+49=83	9+25+64=98	9+36+49=94		

Numbers that can be made are:
14, 21, 26, 29, 30, 35, 38, 41, 42, 45, 46, 49, 50, 53, 54, 56, 59, 61, 62, 65, 66, 69, 70, 74, 75, 77, 78, 81, 83, 84, 86, 89, 90, 91, 93, 94, 98.

MISSION FILE 5:12 Echo proves she 'nose' best!

TM

1) 120 mins = 2 hours

Time	Mrs T and James	Prince B and Echo
40 mins	1 lap	$1\frac{1}{3}$ laps
80 mins	2 laps	$2\frac{2}{3}$ laps
120 mins	3 laps (lapped)	4 laps

2) 2 laps
3) 60 mins = 1 hour

M1

1) 4 times
2) They do 1 lap in 2 hours and travel at 6 km per hour so track = 2 x 6 km = 12 km.
3) They do 1 lap of 12 km in $1\frac{1}{2}$ hours so speed = 12 ÷ 1.5 = 8 km per hour

Da Vinci files

Time	Mrs T and James	Prince B and Echo
80 mins	1 lap	$1\frac{1}{4}$ laps
160 mins	2 laps	$2\frac{1}{2}$ laps
240 mins	3 laps	$3\frac{3}{4}$ laps
300 mins	4 laps (lapped)	5 laps

1) 5 laps (Prince Barrington and Echo do $1\frac{1}{4}$ laps in 80 mins)
2) 4 laps
3) 30 laps (24 x 1.25)

MISSION FILE 5:13 No joy for D. A. F. T. joyriders

TM

1) 36 (11, 22, 33, 44, 55, 66, 77, 88, 99 ,101, 111, 121, 131,141, 151, 161, 171, 181, 191, 202, 212, 222, 232, 242, 252, 262, 272, 282, 292, 303, 313, 323, 333, 343, 353, 363)
2) 49 (those in 1) and 373, 383, 393, 404, 414, 424, 434, 444, 454, 464, 474, 484, 494)

M1

1) 25052 – 24942 = 110 miles
2) 25152 - 25052 = 100 miles, at 60 mph takes 1 hour and 40 mins
From 1 pm this takes the time to 2.40 pm
3) 4.20 pm
4) 25352 25452 25552 25652 25752 25852 25952 26062 26162 26262
26362 26462 26562 26662 26762 26862 26962 27072 27172 27272

Da Vinci files

10.1.01	10.2.01	10.3.01	10.4.01	10.5.01	10.6.01	10.7.01	10.8.01	10.9.01	10.11.01	20.1.02	20.2.02	20.3.02	20.4.02
20.5.02	20.6.02	20.7.02	20.8.02	20.9.02	20.11.02	30.1.03	30.3.03	30.4.03	30.5.03	30.4.03	30.5.03	30.6.03	30.7.03
30.8.03	30.9.03	30.11.03	11.1.11	11.2.11	11.3.11	11.4.11	11.5.11	11.6.11	11.7.11	11.8.11	11.9.11	11.11.11	21.1.12
21.2.12	21.3.12	21.4.12	21.5.12	21.6.12	21.7.12	21.8.12	21.9.12	21.11.12	31.1.13	31.3.13	31.5.13	31.7.13	31.8.13

Gives 56 dates.

Your child may include dates such as 3.1.13. Discuss these and decide whether or not they should be counted as palindromic dates. There is no right answer!

MISSION FILE 5:14 A UFO problem for Victor

TM

1) 6.40 am on 2nd May
2) 4 am on 13th October

M1

1) 1.40 am on 1st January
2) 4 am on 5th January
3) Midnight on 5th May unless it's a leap year, in which case it will be midnight on 4th May.
4) Midnight on 27th October unless it's a leap year, in which case it will be midnight on 26th October.
5) Midnight on 29th July unless it's a leap year, in which case it will be midnight on 28th July.

Da Vinci files

Name	Time needed	Time and date have to start
Andy Mann	6000 secs = 100 mins	10.20 pm on 30th March 2010
Noel Lectric	6000 mins = 100 hours	8 pm on 26th March 2010
Lewis Screw	3000 hours = 125 days	Midnight on 25th November 2009
Anne Nail	300 days	Midnight on 3rd June 2009
Ivor Hammer	30 weeks	Midnight on 1st September 2009

MISSION FILE 5:15 A Major dilemma

Children will need a calculator for this Mission.

TM

1) 2.7 x 39.37 = 106.299 inches = (106.299 ÷ 12) feet = 8.85825 feet
2) 6400 ml = 6.4 litres = (6.4 ÷ 4.546) gallons = 1.408 gallons (3 decimal places)
3) 3.4 kg = 3400 g = 3400 ÷ 28.35 ounces = 119.93 ounces (2 decimal places)

M1

1) 8 miles = 12.88 km
2) 4 yards = 3.656 metres
3) 3 pints = 1.704 litres
4) 9 inches = 0.2286... metres
5) $12m^2$ = 14.354... $yards^2$

Da Vinci files

1) 14 gallons x 4.546 = 63.644 litres = 63 644 ml
2) 12 ounces x 28.35 = 340.2 g = 0.3402 kg

MISSION FILE 5:16 Proportions of portions

Children will need a calculator for this Mission.

TM

16 mins $\rightarrow \frac{1}{4}$, so bus $\rightarrow \frac{3}{4} \rightarrow$ 3 x 16 = 48 mins and total = 16 + 48 = 64 mins

$\frac{1}{4} \rightarrow$ 64 mins, so train $\rightarrow \frac{3}{4} \rightarrow$ 64 x 3 = 192 mins and total = 64 + 192 = 256 mins

$\frac{1}{4} \rightarrow$ = 256 mins, so plane $\rightarrow \frac{3}{4} \rightarrow$ 256 x 3 = 768 and total = 256 + 768 = 1024 mins

1) Train = 192 mins = 3 hours 12 mins
2) Plane – bus = 720 mins = 12 hours
3) Total = 1024 mins = 17 hours 4 mins

M1

$\frac{1}{5} \rightarrow$ 20p, so cola $\rightarrow \frac{4}{5}$ = 80p and total is £1
$\frac{1}{5} \rightarrow$ £1, so fruit salad $\rightarrow \frac{4}{5} \rightarrow$ £4 and total is £5
$\frac{1}{5} \rightarrow$ £5, so cheese salad $\rightarrow \frac{4}{5} \rightarrow$ £20 and total is £25

1) Fruit salad = £4
2) Total at start = £25
   $\frac{1}{6} \rightarrow$ 30p, so orange juice $\rightarrow \frac{5}{6} \rightarrow$ £1.50 and total is £1.80
   $\frac{1}{6} \rightarrow$ £1.80, so garlic bread $\rightarrow \frac{5}{6} \rightarrow$ £9 and total is £10.80
   $\frac{1}{6} \rightarrow$ £10.80, so lasagne $\rightarrow \frac{5}{6} \rightarrow$ £54 and total is £64.80
3) Four orange juices cost £6
4) Started with £64.80

Da Vinci files

Apple juice → $\frac{2}{8}$ → £1.74, so carrot cake → $\frac{6}{8}$ = £5.22 and total = £6.96

£6.96 → 25%, so cabbage casserole → 75% → £20.88 and total is £27.84

$\frac{1}{4}$ → £27.84, so sprout surprise → $\frac{3}{4}$ → £83.52 and total is £111.36

So started with £111.36

MISSION FILE 5:17 Buckett saves the skins of D.A.F.T agents!

TM

1) 1.25 agents a day x 28 days = 35 agents
2) 200 agents ÷ 1.25 agents a day = 160 days = 22 weeks and 6 days

M1

1) $1\frac{1}{8}$ agents in $1\frac{1}{8}$ days so 1 agent in 1 day
   126 agents in 126 days = 18 weeks
2) 1 year and 20 weeks = 365 days and 140 days = 505 days = 505 agents
3) 504 days

Da Vinci files

1) 32 days → 5 spades, so 64 days → 10 spades
2) $\frac{4}{5}$ day → $\frac{1}{8}$ spade, so 4 days → $\frac{5}{8}$ spade
   8 weeks = 56 days
   56 ÷ 4 = 14, so spades = $\frac{5}{8}$ x 14 = $8\frac{3}{4}$ spades.

Sandy would uncover 8 whole spades and $\frac{3}{4}$ of the ninth spade.

MISSION FILE 5:18 An irritating plan

TM

Swimming pool → $\frac{5}{8}$ at 1.30 pm
Bingo → $\frac{3}{4}$ at 1.50 pm, so 20 mins → $\frac{3}{4} - \frac{5}{8} = \frac{6}{8} - \frac{5}{8} = \frac{1}{8}$

1) $\frac{1}{8}$ → 20 mins, so total time = 8 x 20 mins = 160 mins = 2 hours and 40 mins
2) $\frac{1}{8}$ → 20 mins and at 1.30 had gone $\frac{5}{8}$
   $\frac{5}{8}$ → 100 mins = 1 hour and 40 mins
   1.30 pm – 1 hour 40 mins = 11.50 am
3) $\frac{1}{8}$ → 20 mins and at 1.30 pm had gone $\frac{5}{8}$
   $\frac{3}{8}$ left to go = 60 mins = 1 hour
   1.30 pm + 1 hour = 2.30 pm

OR – 11.50 am + 2 hours and 40 mins = 2.30 pm

M1

1) Late
2) 30 minutes late. $\frac{1}{3}$ → 3.07 pm and $\frac{1}{6}$ → 3.17 pm, so $\frac{1}{6}$ = 10 minutes
   $\frac{2}{3}$ to go = 4 x 10 minutes = 40 minutes so time will be 3.17 pm + 40 minutes = 3.57 pm
   The watch is 3 minutes slow making the time 4 pm, so they are 30 minutes late.
3) Late
4) 24 minutes
   $\frac{1}{5}$ → 11.35 am and $\frac{1}{4}$ = 11.51 am, so $\frac{1}{20}$ = 16 minutes
   $\frac{1}{4}$ = 5 x 16 minutes = 80 minutes
   $\frac{3}{4}$ to go = 3 x 80 minutes = 240 minutes (4 hours)
   So time will be 11.51 am + 240 minutes = 3.51 pm
   The watch is 3 minutes slow making the time 3.54 pm so 24 minutes late.

Da Vinci files

1) Early
2) $\frac{2}{3}$ → 2.08 pm and $\frac{3}{4}$ → 2.17 pm so $\frac{1}{12}$ = 9 minutes
   $\frac{1}{4}$ = 3 x 9 minutes = 27 minutes to go
   So time will be 2.17 pm + 27 minutes = 2.44 pm
   The watch is 3 minutes slow, making the time 2.47 pm so 43 minutes early.

M1

If you can find the maximum number of consecutive numbers which total these numbers, Stella may well win a few thousand pounds from Saturday's draw!

1) What is the maximum number of consecutive numbers that can be added together to make 142?

2) Try 186.

3) How about 243?

4) Try 367.

Sterling work! If Stella can complete the Da Vinci Challenge, she may just be lucky enough to scoop the jackpot!

Da Vinci files

1) Investigate the maximum number of consecutive numbers that can be added to give a FOUR-digit number?

2) Can multiplying a set of consecutive numbers give a total of 120?

3) Investigate the maximum number of consecutive numbers that can be multiplied to give THREE-, FOUR-, FIVE-, and SIX-digit numbers?

Huxley's Think Tank

You may find to helpful to remember that:

Odd + Odd = Even

Even + Even = Even

Even + Odd = Odd

On your bike, Tex!

Time: After supper
Place: Tex's office

President Maryland 'Tex' Wordsworth of the U.S.A has been saving up to buy a new mountain bike for absolutely ages! Unfortunately, his calculator, which he needs to work out how much he has left to save, has developed a fault.

Every time he types in a THREE-digit number, the calculator screen flashes up with a SINGLE-digit number. When he types in the number 369 the screen displays the number 2. It's time for Brain Academy to step in.

TM

For example:

597 ➜ 5 x 9 x 7 = 315
315 ➜ 3 x 1 x 5 = 15
15 ➜ 1 x 5 = 5

1) How many THREE-digit numbers below 200 can you find with a 'blip' of 2?

2) How many can you find with a blip of 5?

M1

If Tex can answer these questions he'll be able to buy his dream bike.

1) Which SINGLE-digit 'blip' can be most easily made from a THREE-digit number below 200?

2) How many ways can you find to make it?

3) Can you make a 'blip' of all the numbers from 0-9 using any THREE-digit numbers?

4) Can you make a 'blip' of all the numbers from 0-9 using FOUR-digit numbers?

5) Investigate making 'blips' of the numbers 0-9 using FIVE and SIX-digit numbers. Try to make as many digits as possible greater than one.

Completing the Da Vinci Challenge will mean that Tex will be able go cycling with his friends next weekend.

Da Vinci files

What happens when you try and find the 'blip' of a number whose digits are consecutive?

Rows and rows of roses

Time: After breakfast
Place: An empty flower bed

A group of D.A.F.T. agents have decided to dampen Valentine's Day celebrations by 'plotting' an evil plan to pick every single red rose in England. Echo the Eco-Warrior has agreed to help bring romance back to the country by planting bulbs where those beautiful bushes once blossomed.

TM

Echo is to fill TWO flower beds with roses. She must plant a square array of bulbs in each bed. Help her to work out which square number of bulbs must be planted in EACH bed to equal the total amount of bulbs that she has been given.

1) Echo has 34 bulbs. She must plant a square number in each of the TWO flower beds to form TWO different square arrays of bulbs. How many must she plant in each flower bed?

2) If the total number of bulbs is 72, how many must she plant in each flower bed to form TWO square arrays?

3) What if the total number of bulbs is 116?

M1

It won't be long before these roses of yours are looking 'blooming' marvellous, Echo. If Valentine's Day is to be a success you will need to keep planting! Can you help Echo by answering these questions?'

Echo can't decide how to plant some or all of her 100 bulbs in square arrays in TWO flower beds.

1) **Find all the whole numbers from 1 to 100 that can be written as the sum of TWO different square numbers, so Echo will know how many options she has.**

2) **How can you be sure you have found all the possibilities?**

Beautiful work! If Echo can take the Da Vinci Challenge the flowers will bloom and Echo will have saved the day for all you romantics!

Da Vinci files

When you are certain that you have found all the whole numbers that can be written as the sum of TWO different square numbers, investigate the whole numbers, from 1 to 100, that are the sum of THREE different square numbers.

MISSION FILE 5:12

Echo proves she 'nose' best!

Time: 3.00pm
Place: Echo's park

Numbers of North American Tree Skunks are falling and these smelly creatures will soon be wiped out for good. These rare creatures are set to become ex-stink! Echo hopes to raise enough cash to sponsor some skunks by holding a three-legged race!

TM

It takes Prince Barrington and Echo half an hour to stagger round the block. It takes Mrs Tiggles and James Bond 40 minutes.

1) If they were to keep going, how long would it be before Mrs Tiggles and her pet are lapped?

2) What if Mrs Tiggles had a head start and began exactly half way round the block. How many laps would it take the Prince and Echo to catch her?

3) How long would this take?

M1

All the characters are at the starting line. Echo needs your help in deciding who wins, if the race is to be a success.

1) It takes Prince Barrington and Echo 90 minutes to do a lap. It takes Mrs Tiggles and James 120 minutes to complete a lap. How many times will Prince Barrington and Echo have to go round the track before they catch up with Mrs Tiggles?

2) If Mrs Tiggles and James are travelling at an average speed of 6km per hour, how long is a lap?

3) Can you work out how fast Prince Barrington and Echo are travelling?

Excellent! To save those skunks, Echo must take the Da Vinci Challenge.

Da Vinci files

It takes Mrs Tiggles and James 80 minutes to complete a lap and it takes the Prince and Echo 64 minutes.

1) How many laps will the Prince and Echo have done before they meet again?
2) How many laps will Mrs Tiggles and James have done?

If Mrs Tiggles maintains her pace, it will take her 32 hours to complete 24 laps.

3) How many laps will the Prince and Echo have done after this time?

No joy for D.A.F.T. joyriders

Time: Mid-afternoon
Place: A stolen fire engine

Sandy Buckett has a passion for palindromic numbers. So much so that she has programmed her fire engine radio to give a blast of the song 'London's Burning' every time the mileometer shows a palindromic number. You can imagine how shocked two D.A.F.T. joyriders must have felt when the engine that they had stolen that morning kept blaring out this tedious tune. Mrs Tiggles wants to help and is in hot pursuit in her shopping trolly.

TM

1) The mileometer shows that the vehicle has travelled 365 km. How many times would they have heard the song play?

2) They continue driving for another 129 km. How many times would they have heard the song in total?

M1

Answering these palindromic problems will guarantee the arrest of the agents. Mrs Tiggles can't manage this mission on her own. Are you ready?

1) The mileometer showed that the fire engine had done a total of 24942 miles. How much further have the two D.A.F.T. agents driven when, at 1pm, they hear 'London's Burning' playing and notice another palindromic number on the dashboard?

2) If the agents keep driving at a constant speed of 60 miles per hour, what time will it be when the mileometer shows another palindromic number?

3) If they keep driving at the same constant speed, what time will it be when they hear the next blast of the song?

4) What will the next TWENTY palindromic numbers be?

Well done! Completing the Da Vinci Challenge will mean that Mrs Tiggles can get the joyriders arrested and drive the engine back to Sandy.

Da Vinci files

How many palindromic dates will we have in the first 20 years of the next millennium?

Take the first year as 3001.
Record the dates in the form 1.3.08

MISSION FILE 5:14

A UFO problem for Victor

Time: 31 Dec 2004. 11.55pm
Place: NASA headquarters

Sightings of Unidentified Floating Objects off the coast of 'Mansend' are causing panic across the nation. Victor Blastov has agreed to help the Ministry of Defence design and build a submarine to investigate these inexplicable inflatables.

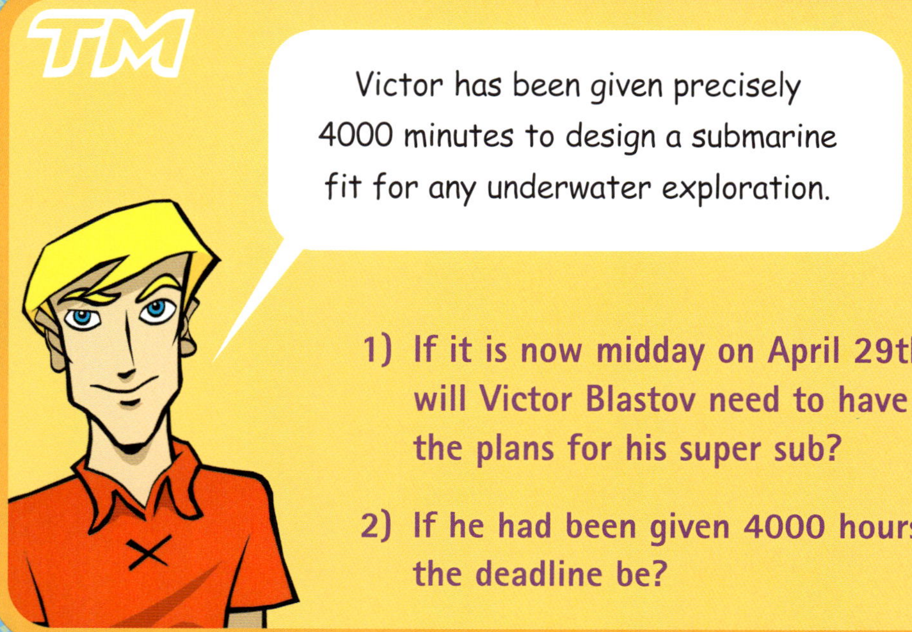

1) If it is now midday on April 29th, when will Victor Blastov need to have completed the plans for his super sub?

2) If he had been given 4000 hours when would the deadline be?

M1

It's December 31st and the plans have been accepted! Victor designates a task to each of his FIVE engineers but he needs your help in working out at what time of what day they'll be finished. (There are no leap years involved!)

1) From the second the clock strikes midnight, it will be exactly 6000 seconds until Andy Mann completes the periscope. When will the periscope be ready?

2) From the second the clock strikes midnight, it will be exactly 6000 minutes until Noel Lectric wires up the lighting. When will the lights come on?

3) From the second the clock strikes midnight, it will be exactly 3000 hours before Lewis Screw organises the oxygen. When will the air become breathable in the sub?

4) From the second the clock strikes midnight, it will be exactly 300 days until Anne Nail installs radar. When will their radar start to work?

5) From the second the clock strikes midnight it will be exactly 30 weeks until Ivor Hammer fits the spoiler. When will the spoiler be in position?

Great work Team! If Victor can take the Da Vinci Challenge the country can be saved from these Unidentified Floating Objects!

Da Vinci files

The deadline for completion of the submarine is midnight on 30th March 2010. If each of the engineers is to finish as the clock strikes midnight on this date, when must the work begin?

A Major Dilemma

Time: 11.46am exactly
Place: BA headquarters

Sergeant Major Dilemma is concerned that his soldiers aren't fit enough. He has called for the help of his old friend, General Cods-Wallop, to help design a new assault course that will improve the fitness of these saggy soldiers.

The problem is that Sergeant Major Dilemma understands Metric measure, where as this is all cods-wallop to the General, who is used to the old fashioned, Imperial units of measure.

TM

To convert pints to litres – multiply by 0.568
To convert ounces to grams – multiply by 28.35
To convert metres to inches – multiply by 39.37
To convert feet to centimetres – multiply by 30.48
To convert miles to kilometres – multiply by 1.61
To convert yards to metres – multiply by 0.914
To convert gallons to litres – multiply by 4.546
To convert square yards to square metres – multiply by 0.836

1) How many feet in 2.7 m?

2) How many gallons in 6400 ml?

3) How many ounces in 3.4 kg?

M1

Can you work out which TWO units the men are talking about in each of these statements? Answering these questions will mean that the assault course can be built next week.

1) 8 of mine is 12.88 of yours.

2) 4 of mine is 3.656 of yours.

3) 3 of mine is 1.704 of yours.

4) 9 of mine is 0.229 of yours.

5) 12 of mine is 14.35 of yours.

Attention! Completing the Da Vinci Challenge will mean that those soldiers will become the fittest, toughest fighting machine in the land.

Da Vinci files

Which TWO units are involved in each of these statements?

1) 14 of mine is 63644 of yours.

2) 12 of mine is 0.340 of yours.

Huxley's Think Tank

All may not be quite as it seems! Don't forget about how many millilitres are equivalent to a litre or how many grams are in a kilogram.

Proportions of portions

Time: Lunchtime
Place: A restaurant in England

President Maryland T Wordsworth is extremely worried that too few Americans are eating five portions of fruit and veg each day. Tex feels that the huge number of 'Mc Chubby's' burger bars in every high street are to blame, so has promised to travel to England to take a leaf from the English eateries and educate the folks back home.

TM

Tex spent $\frac{3}{4}$ of his total travelling time on the plane.
Then he spent $\frac{3}{4}$ of the remaining journey time on the train.
He then spent $\frac{3}{4}$ of the remaining journey time on the bus.
He spent the last 16 minutes walking.

1) How long did he spend on the train?

2) How much longer did he spend on the plane than the bus?

3) How long was the total journey?

M1

Answering these questions will ensure that Tex picks up some healthy eating tips to take back home.

Tex went to the popular restaurant, 'Salad City'.
He spent $\frac{4}{5}$ of his money on a cheese salad.
He spent $\frac{4}{5}$ of the money that was left on a fruit salad.
He spent $\frac{4}{5}$ of what was left on a diet coke.
He spent his last 20p on some bread and butter.

1) How much was the fruit salad?
2) How much money did he start with?

Tex also ate at 'Pasta Palace' with his staff.
He spent $\frac{5}{6}$ of his money on lasagne.
He spent $\frac{5}{6}$ of what was left on garlic bread.
He spent $\frac{5}{6}$ of what was left on an orange juice.
He tipped the waitress with the last remaining 30p.

3) How much would FOUR orange juices cost?
4) How much money did he start with?

Terrific! Completing the Da Vinci Challenge will ensure that people tuck into five portions of fruit and veg every day!

Da Vinci files

Tex ate at 'Vegetable Village'.
He spent $\frac{3}{4}$ of his money on a sprout surprise.
He spent 75% of what was left on a cabbage casserole.
He spent $\frac{6}{8}$ of what was left on a slice of carrot cake.
He spent his last remaining £1.74 on a freshly squeezed apple juice.
How much money did he start with?

MISSION FILE 5:17

Buckett saves the skins of D.A.F.T. agents!

Time: 9.00am
Place: 'Bestgos' supermarket

A group of D.A.F.T. agents have decided to put a dampener on the summer barbecue season by stealing sausages from a well-known supermarket. They dug underneath the supermarket to take the store by surprise but have got stuck. Luckily, Sandy Buckett has been called to come and save their skins!

TM

1) If the fire brigade free one and a quarter D.A.F.T. agents in a day how many agents will they have rescued in FOUR weeks?

2) How many weeks and how many days would it take them to rescue 200 D.A.F.T. agents?

M1

Sandy is going to rescue the rest of the robbers but she needs your help to work out how long it will take.

1) If it takes Sandy's team a day and an eighth to uncover one whole and one eighth of an agent, how long would it take them to rescue 126 agents?

2) If they were to dig for one year and 20 weeks how many agents would they uncover?

3) How long would it take the fire brigade to uncover 504 D.A.F.T. agents?

Excellent! If Sandy can see this Da Vinci Challenge through, she'll uncover those undercover agents and hand them over to Buster Crimes.

Da Vinci files

Sandy needs to find the incriminating spades in order to get enough evidence to convict the D.A.F.T. agents. It takes her $\frac{4}{5}$ of a day to uncover $\frac{1}{8}$ of a spade.

1) How long would it take her to uncover TEN spades.

2) How many would she uncover in EIGHT weeks?

An irritating plan

Time: 2.00pm exactly
Place: Dr Hood's office

Dr Hood is busy plotting his latest scam to irritate the nation. He wants to send people potty by sprinkling itching powder across the country. Buster Crimes decides that he should be the one to stop these annoying agents!

Where shall I start, Da Vinci?

Huxley has a Training Mission that will sooth your nerves and calm that itch!

TM

In order to gain enough evidence to lock up the agents, Buster needs to work out their schedule.

Buster followed a group of D.A.F.T. agents as they walked from Dr Hood's office to the joke shop. They passed the swimming pool at 1.30pm. They had completed five eighths of their journey. At 1.50pm they passed the BINGO hall. This was three quarters of the way into their journey.

1) How long did the journey take from the office of Dr Hood to the joke shop?

2) What time did they leave?

3) What time did they arrive?

M1

Buster was spying on the agents very closely indeed. Answering these questions will allow him to arrest the villains.

Buster is looking through the window of Dr Hood's office. This is what he sees:

Dr Hood looks at the clock in his office; the time is exactly 2.00pm.

"Do any of you have a watch?" asks Hood. One of the agents checks his watch, which is exactly three minutes slow. "Make sure that you're all back here by 3.30pm at the latest, or there will be serious trouble."

The agents manage to buy the itching powder relatively easily and so decide to stop off at the local 'Mc Chubby's' for a snack.

They become worried that they are going to be late so start to head back to the office.

As they reach Red Deer Park they know they have completed a sixth of the return journey. The agent in charge of time-keeping looked at his watch. It said 3.07pm. As they walk past the cinema, the same watch shows that the time is 3.17pm. The agents have now completed a third of their journey back.

1) Will the agents make it on time or will they be late?
2) Work out exactly how many minutes early or late the irritating idiots are.

The next day they visit another joke shop. On their way back to the office they reach the village teashop when the faulty watch says 11.35am. They have completed one fifth of their journey. As they walk past the bus garage the watch shows that it is nine minutes before midday. They have completed one quarter of the journey.

3) Will they arrive back late or early?
4) By how many minutes?

Excellent! Completing the Da Vinci Challenge will ensure the D.A.F.T. agents are arrested before they can sprinkle a speck of itching powder.

Da Vinci files

Later that week they visit yet another joke shop. On their return journey they reach Joe's Café when the faulty watch says 2.08pm. They have completed two thirds of their journey. As they walk past the church the watch shows that it is 2.17pm. They have completed three quarters of the journey.

1) Will they arrive back late or early?
2) By how many minutes?

Mission Strategies 1

Use the TASC Problem-solving Wheel to guide you through the Mission Files. It will help you to become more confident and think of ideas for yourself. You might find it helpful to start at *Gather/organise* and work clockwise around the Wheel using the questions to help you think through each problem.

Reflect
What have I learned?

Communicate
Who can I tell?

Evaluate
Did I succeed? Can I think of another way?

Implement
Now let me do it!

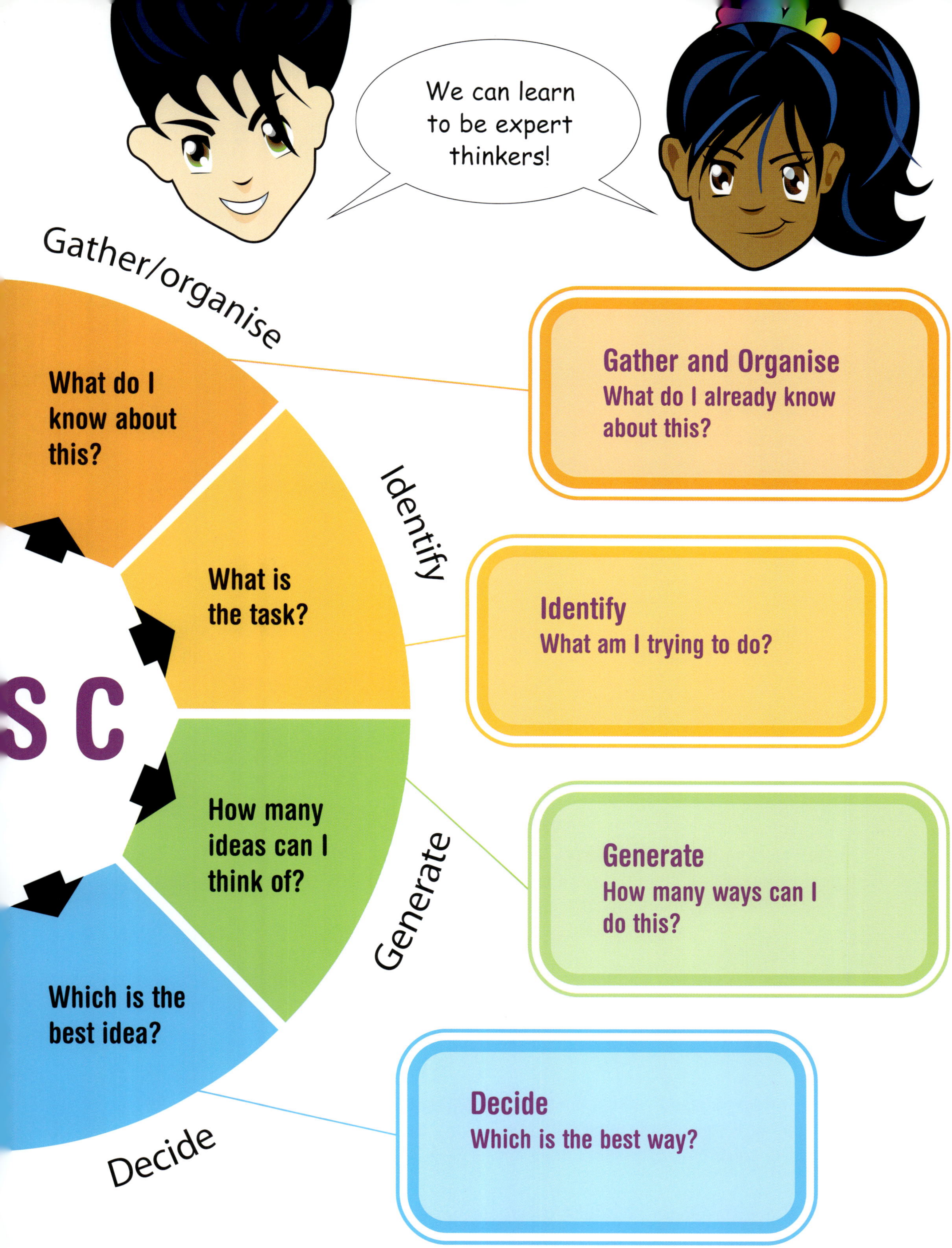
We can learn to be expert thinkers!
Gather/organise
What do I know about this?
Identify
What is the task?
S C
Generate
How many ideas can I think of?
Decide
Which is the best idea?
Gather and Organise
What do I already know about this?
Identify
What am I trying to do?
Generate
How many ways can I do this?
Decide
Which is the best way?

Mission Strategies 2

MISSION FILE 5:1

These are tricky questions, so start by identifying what you are have to do. Talk about your answers with a friend – this will help you to see whether you have got the method correct. CLUE: think in spirals!

MISSION FILE 5:2

Remember; you should have as few doors as possible but each truck must be able to get out! Drawing up diagrams on squared paper will be helpful here.

MISSION FILE 5:3

Use what you have already learnt about fractions to help you work through this Mission File. This will be of use when you tackle other similar activities.

MISSION FILE 5:4

How many ways are there to do this Mission File? Using three measuring jugs will get you started, but can using any particular calculations help you as well?

MISSION FILE 5:5

Use a table to help you answer these questions. Put the runners at the top and the positions they finished down the side. When you know that Charlotte has come first, cross off Maureen, Anne and Jenny as they can't all finish in this position.

MISSION FILE 5:6

You are going to have to make equivalent fractions to complete this mission. Look for the lowest common denominator. SUPER CLUE: Think 3 x 10 for TM1!

MISSION FILE 5:7

Before starting the TM think about how to orgainse your working process. You could estimate first and then work out the answer from there, or work step–by–step (1 + 2 + 3 + 4…). Use whichever method suits you best.

MISSION FILE 5:8

Remember the squares can be made up of more than one piece. This is important if you are going to get all the combinations. Drawing pictures or breaking up your own chocolate bar will help!

MISSION FILE 5:9

In the Training Mission, divide the total by the number of consecutive numbers. An odd number of consecutive numbers must divide with no remainder and an even number of consecutive numbers must end in xx.5 for it to work!

MISSION FILE 5:10

In the Da Vinci Files there is a rule for blips that you should try to find out. Start with simple consecutive numbers 123, 234 and so on to keep the mathematics simple.

MISSION FILE 5:11

You must work logically and in order so you don't miss any possibilities. Draw a couple of square arrays to help you visualise the problem more clearly.

MISSION FILE 5:12

Use the Training Mission to work out your method. Then write it down and see if you and your friends can follow the same method for Mission 1. You could even set up your own race to check your answers!

MISSION FILE 5:13

Some palindromic number examples are 121, 12.4.21, 65756 km. These numbers read the same backwards as forwards. Eye, radar and madam are three great word palindromes!

MISSION FILE 5:14

Write down what you know: 24 hours = 1440 minutes = 86400 seconds. Bear in mind that the number of days in each month change too.

MISSION FILE 5:15

To keep the answers accurate always round your final answer to 2 decimal places but don't do any rounding before the last stage of your calculations.

MISSION FILE 5:16

Work out what $\frac{1}{4}$, $\frac{1}{5}$ and $\frac{1}{6}$ are first. This information will enable you to answer the questions accurately. Keep your working this simple and you can't fail!

MISSION FILE 5:17

Here is a good strategy to get you thinking mathematically. Convert all the words you've been given into figures and re-write the questions. What are you really being asked to find out?

MISSION FILE 5:18

In M1 there is a lot of reading. Make notes of the key facts and information before starting work and have a clock or watch to hand. The questions are asking for different types of answers (words and numbers) so be aware of this as you work. Revisit your notes at the end to see if they helped.

nace

What is NACE?

NACE is an independent charity set up in 1984. It supports the teaching of more able learners and helps all children to find out what they are good at and to do their best.

What does NACE do?

NACE helps teachers by giving them advice, books, materials and training. Many teachers, headteachers, parents and governors join NACE. The NACE website gives its members useful advice, ideas and materials to help children to learn.

How will this book help me?

The Brain Academy Maths books challenge and help you to become better at learning and a better mathematician by:

- thinking of and testing different solutions to problems;
- making connections to what you already know;
- making mistakes and learning from them;
- working by yourself and with others;
- expecting you to get better and to go on to the next book;
- learning skills which you can use in other subjects and out of school.

We hope that you enjoy the books!

RISING STARS

Rising Stars Ltd, 7 Hatchers Mews, Bermondsey Street, London SE1 3GS